GUILTY ESCAPE

ALEX GERARDO

Charleston, SC
www.PalmettoPublishing.com

Guilty Escape
Copyright © 2020 by Alex Gerardo

All rights reserved

Paperback: 978-1-64990-646-5
Hardback (Case): 978-1-64990-647-2
eBook: 978-1-64990-644-1

To my boys, John, Victor, and Damien.

INTRO-

WRITE:

Write
Write it down,
Breath.

The only way to calm myself
Is to feel the glide of my pen on paper.
To see the imperfect English language manipulated to fit
the thoughts in my head
The spinning room clears and the screams calm down
But only as the ink covers the page
Filling it with the deepest parts of who I am.

I'm a writer
Nothing less, nothing more
A person able to take the same twenty-six characters
people see every day
Make them feel what I'm feeling
See what I'm saying
Understand the world through my own eyes

It's the only way to make these voices stop
They scream
They tear at everything around me

"You're not enough"
"You don't try hard enough"

"You only pretend to care"
"No one loves you
They only help because they have to"
"People are only your friend because they feel sorry for
you"

They are the voices of my friends
My family
My demons
They are all I hear

But as soon as my pen touches the paper
Calm
The voices around me disappear
They let me breathe again
The throbbing in my head lessening to a bearable amount
Never gone
But enough to finish each day

ACT 1– ESCAPE

When I first started writing, it was mostly fiction
Tall tales of princesses and heroes
Love and loss
It was a way of escaping my world into one of my own making
But as my life started to change and things started getting worse
My fantasy worlds started shifting before my eyes
The hero lost
The princess turned on her savior
Even the knight in shining armor had dark secrets
The real world started leaking into my imaginary ones
Running their streets with blood and betrayal

RELEASE:

As the beat pulses
The lights glow brighter
A beam of blue
An aura of red
Slow-moving gems of white light dancing over the bodies
of those in the crowd
She watches as her lover's soul seems to float above her
body

Each song blends into the next
The DJ was their God
And them his humble servants
The pound of the bass vibrated the floor under their feet
The melody flooding their veins with heat and lust and
power

The air was thick with the smell of booze and sweat
But no one seemed to mind
It reminded them most of the smell of freedom

The music lifts her chest to the ceiling
And brings her spirit out of her and into the fog above the
crowd

No longer a crowd of individuals
But a sea of color and motion

So vivid it burned to stare at it all for too long
But too beautiful to look away from

It all fades to nothingness
As their physical forms become obsolete

All that matters is the collective feeling of release
A unified braking of societal chains

No more worries
No responsibility
No trying to fit in
No trying to stand out
The universe can disappear and leave them in this moment forever
And not one of them would notice
Nor would they care if they did
This is the new meaning of life

CONSUMED:

Red Orange Yellow White Blue
Dancing Flickering Caressing
A crackle
A Whisper

"You can burn too
Burn with me
Together we could shine so bright"

As I watched
I could feel her burn
Deep
Dry
Heat
Resonating from within her
Powerful and bright

But as her flames grew
She shrank inside of them
Her face a mix of malice and pain
Each time she raised her arms
Her skin flaked off into embers and ash
The smell of something foul and charred catching in the
wind

She was running out of time
She had no other option
She tried to escape it
To separate herself from it
Before it consumed her completely

But each time she grew smaller
Weaker
Until she found someone new to pull in with her
To believe her lies and tricks
And once she had enough fuel she would begin to grow
again

A GIFT AND A CURSE:

His eyes were the most memorable part of him
The ocean freezing over in the dead of winter
Piercing even the strongest armor
They saw past everything
All the scars
All the burns
All impurities

He never saw my veins
Stark against my porcelain skin
He never noticed how my collar bone stuck out
Sharp yet fragile
He never noticed my scars and scabs and bruises
His eyes skipped over it all
Only seeing the parts of me that I wanted people to see
A pure
Whole
Unblemished version of me

They filled your heart
Your soul
Made you feel whole
By filling your emptiness with empathy and love

But no gift is free
Eventually, his eyes move on

Taking with them that fullness
Leaving you with a bigger hole then you started with

He will fill someone else

And I paid that price with what was left of my soul
There will be a hole
Forever empty
Surrounding my heart
A chasm in my chest

THE WATCHER:

Behind the glass was a girl with no name. Her job was to watch. She saw all there was. She could never talk, never join, never explore. Only watch. The girl was tasked with this job thousands of years ago, it was up to her to make sure we stayed safe; that we followed the rules. She was the one who told Him if we'd been bad or good. She warned Him when we needed to be taught a lesson.

Only one human had ever been able to see her. He was looking for a second chance, a redemption of sorts.

Instead, all he got was a quest of fate that would lead to his entrapment. The day he found the Watcher was the day that she died, and he took her place for the next thousand years.

TRAPPED:

One breath at a time
Ice forms in the air around my face as the wind pushes to
isolate me
I lost the feeling in my fingers long ago
My heart no longer pumps blood
But instead pushes slush through my veins
Movement is pointless
I am pointless

He sits on the other side of the glass watching me with
intent eyes
What does he want from me?
I have no money
No family
Nothing I can give him but the apparent amusement of
my suffering

My fingers go numb
Turning red
to blue
to black
I can't feel my nose
I can't move my lips
What is he looking for
Why won't he make this end

Then warmth.
Burning
Fire
My body is light
Hot
White light
A light that never stops
My veins melt
Now pumping lava
My bones are made of the sun
My brain feels nothing

Freedom

MY SAVIOR:

His shadow was lean
Tall
Thin
With some kind of hood over his head
Black and stark against the colorful sky
I never saw his face
It was like he was afraid to show himself

I would see him riding down the road
On my bike down 5s
The occasional house or farm passing by on either side of
me
He would be there
Hiding amongst the trees
Or in the fields
Or in the cars that passed by me

I would see him in the darkness of my room in the middle
of the night
As I woke from my latest nightmare
Tortured screams caught in my throat

Or he would be there
On nights my dad was really bad
Nights full of yelling
Glass shattering

Mom crying
Pleading

I would see him in the halls of my high school
Always around the corner
Lurking

But I wasn't scared of my shadow man
He was my savior
A sort of guardian angel

My friends all thought I was crazy
They said I was seeing things
But I knew he was real
I hoped

I knew that someday he'd reach out from the shadows
And take me away from this hell
And into the life I deserved
Because unlike my friends and family
My savior loved me

LUCIFER:

An angel fallen from heaven above
Forced to live among those on earth
Forced to hide the scars of his once-great wings
Never feeling at peace
Never fully feeling welcome
Never able to go home

I SOLD MY SOUL:

I sold my soul to the devil for a friend
I was lonely
The demons were angry with me at first
Then understanding
I just wanted someone to talk to
Someone to listen

My parents won't
And if they did
They would get mad
Dad would yell
Slam things
Throw things
Mom would cry
Put her head in her hands and ask her God for help
And I would feel guilty
So guilty
For making them feel this way
I always feel like I shouldn't have said anything in the end

I have people I consider friends
But I wouldn't be able to tell them
They wouldn't understand
Nor would they care
They have their own problems

So I cried out for anyone that would listen
And in my small bedroom that could barely fit my bed
The devil appeared
Angry and roaring
Demanding an explanation

Behind my hands, I sobbed
Scared but determined
I told him of my fears
Of my long lost hopes
And he took pity on me

He offered me his long-clawed hand and took me to a
place no one could hurt me
He showed me his demons
And taught me that they weren't so scary once you con-
fronted them
Then before he sent me home he told me that if I ever
needed someone to talk to
I could reach out for him again

EMPTINESS:

These tears rolling down my face
Aren't the only part of me spilling out
My chest explodes and collapses with every beat
Pouring rotten, tainted blood with it

All the hate and anger thrown at me from every direction
accumulates in my heart
All the backhanded comments
The lies
The harsh truths

My mom thinks pointing out my shortcomings will show
me the better version of myself that I can be
But instead it just reminds me of how much of a disap-
pointment I am to her

And once at school I am surrounded by an immense
pressure
To fit in
To stand out
To fall in love
But not to the woman I love
To be good
To be smart
But not too good
Or too smart

Because then I won't fit in

To let go of that rotted blood
To let it ooze out of me would be a crime
It would pollute those around me
My family

My friends
The people trying to help me

But to keep it in would mean death
It would fill my soul and heart and dissolve them with its
acidity

On days it's really bad
The days where the world is too much to handle
I feel as if I should let it out
But stand inside of a bucket as I do
And do my best to collect these harsh feelings
Collect this poison inside of me
So on days where I feel nothing
Absolutely nothing at all
I can bathe in my blood
In hopes that I could at least feel my past pain

But there are other days
Days where my feelings are too much
Too much suffering

Days I truly realize that I am alone
That all rationale goes to waste
And I wish to everything above me
That I can go back to feeling nothing at all
Because maybe I have a chance
As long as I'm just an empty shell

BLACK VEINS:

Thick black lines trace her veins
From her heart
To the very tips of her fingers and toes
They act as a reminder
A constant symbol
Of the blood forever flowing beneath her skin
Keeping her alive
Through the hardest and most difficult parts of her
journey

The lines started as a hobby
That turned into a habit
That became an imperfection to who she was

For every time she felt her heartache
She would trace a part of her veins
The worse the pain
The darker the line
At the end of each week
She washed her heartache away
And watched as it flowed down the drain

But
Before she even finished the first month of this ritual
The ink no longer washed away
The lines had become too dark

Too deep
Too meaningful to ever let her forget

Now she lives with them
For the rest of her journey
Forever reminded of her pain

And that her blood still flows through her now black
veins

They stand out stark against her snow, white skin
The days of sun and smiles
The lines stand between her and those around her
On days of cold and sorrow
They remind others of how dark emotions can feel

But to her they bring hope
A reminder of where she's been
How far she's come
And how far she can go

When she meets someone new
They ask her where the lines came from
What happened
Why she would mutilate such beautiful skin

She answers with a tale of a girl struggling to find herself
But in the end they only listen so they can move on
They never care for her to explain

ACT 2– MY LOST GIRL

She made everything better
She helped to stop the panic attracts
She held me
She calmed me down
She helped me to understand the world a little bit better

On days filled with rain and clouds
She taught me to appreciate mother nature
To stop
And to watch the storm
To let the rain wash over me

A field full of weeds was a perfect spot for a picnic
A snow day was great for a movie marathon
And the assholes in school weren't worth our time
Nor our thoughts

I trusted her with my whole self
I gave her my heart
I believed fully that she had given me hers

The two of us against the world
Isn't that the saying
We had plans for the future
Loving each other
Living together

No one between us
Within each other's arms
Years going by
Just the two of us
You had me at hello
And held on forevermore

KISS ME NOW:

Would you ever kiss me
One day
Laying in the snow together
Us laughing as we point out the clouds
Would you kiss me then
Would you turn your head and press your lips to my own

Would you ever kiss me
Up late at night
Sitting by the fire
Tears spill out of our long reddened eyes
As we cling to each other for comfort
Would you kiss me then
Would you take away the pain

Would you ever kiss me
Take my hand as we run the bases
Bat and glove on the ground
We play for fun
No real winners
But there's still a rush seeing your smile
As I slide to home base
Would you kiss me then
Would you congratulate me in the only way that feels
right

Would you ever kiss me
Hold me tight as we both dance
Together
Under the glowing lights
Our eyes meet
Shimmering with the excitement of the night
Would you kiss me then
Would you pull me close
Show me the world through your eyes

No
You wouldn't
Because I never asked you to

OUR LOVE WAS FIRE:

Fierce and untamable
Full of raw
Unnameable emotions
With so many words gone unspoken
During soft kisses
And late-night sneaking

No one could know
We burned bright
But low
And with soft crackles
Rather than a roar
Our love was only to be seen by each other's eyes

But it got old fast
Was I not good enough
For you
For your friends

You would snuff me out
Say it was all in my head

But then you put your body to mine
Your mouth would tell me it was all worth the lies
The deceit
All until I was alone again

No one to hold on to
No one to hold me
Cold and burnt out
By myself in the growing hours of the night

I lied to everyone for you!
For us...
It didn't mean anything to you in the end

But then you'd kiss me
And tell me that it would be alright
And I believe you

That was my fault
I believed it
And we would burn together again

EASIER TO HATE:

It was so much easier to yell and scream at her
To get emotional
And to tell each other how much we hated the other
"You ruined me!
You ruined my life
Everything was so much easier before you showed up
So much simpler
I wish I never met you!"

It was easier to say these things than to admit the truth

I loved her
I loved her more than any high schooler should ever love
anyone
She was my Annabel Lee
The light to my darkness
The reason I took each breath
And got out of bed in the morning
She made my miserable life worth living
To see her smile
To hear her laugh
To watch as her hair glowed in the light of each new day

I wanted nothing more than to leave with her
Then and there
Disappear and never look back

Be alone together
No bullies
No bigots
No unresponsive unloving parents
No more expectations

But we lived in the real world
We both knew we were going to get hurt by what we had

And if it weren't for the fighting
We wouldn't care
We couldn't
It would be too real
Too fast
Too terrifying to face

Our hearts hurt after we uttered hateful truths
But that was nothing compared to how it felt
When we told each other how much we were needed
How we couldn't survive the minutes apart
But we couldn't get what we wanted

Heartbreak hurts for a few months before we can both
move on
Forbidden love in a world not ready for its power
That love aches in your heart forever
Filled with its possibilities

It was easier to fight
So we did

DIVERGENCE:

It felt as if something always divided them
The fence between them now was no different
They weren't going to let everyone else win this time
One clung to the others hand
The metal biting into her skin
She would still never let go
She didn't think she could
If everyone wanted to separate them
Then they would have to kill them both
And even then their spirits would dance together through
the sky
That was until the hand she was clinging to
Let go

THE PREDATOR:

Would you watch as my blood flows down my skin
Would you look away
Oblivious
As it pools around me in a puddle of grief and sorrow

Would you cover my bruises
Wrap them without question
Kiss them
Make them better

Would you turn away
Ignore the world around you
Until you forget that I needed your help in the first place

Or will you slowly disappear
Into the wind
Leaving me to die
Alone
In pain

Who are you
Who is the person behind the mask
All kind eyes and strong smiles
Are you something ravenous and festering
A predator on the hunt for your next victim

You were a lie
I trusted you
I gave everything
All of my heart and soul
And you treated me like nothing
You watched as I got worse

As I plunged deeper into a prison of my own making
Did you ever mean the words you said

You didn't
Did you
You lead me on so you could use me for your own
pleasure
You allowed me to give you all that I had left
And you took it with a twisted smile and your fingers
crossed behind your back

Will I ever get to meet you
The real you
I know I won't recognize the person I see
You had always been the person-
NO
The monster
My friends warned me about

MISSING YOU:

She's gone.
I was supposed to tell her not to go
To stay with me
Here, in our own self-made prison
But I couldn't
This was her dream come true
Who was I to stop her from leaving

I'm just going to have to struggle through
Miss her
Love her
Forgive
Then try to forget her
The love of my life was moving on
Living the way she always wanted to

While I stayed behind
Same life
Same story
No real past
No real future
It hurts to know that I'll never be as
Smart
Kind
Wise
As she is

I can try
But I'll fail

It's so hard not to miss her
I see her in everything I do
Everywhere I go
I wish when she left
She took my memories with her
It'd be so much easier to get over her if she were gone for
good

TIME WON'T GO BY:

How many times do you refresh the page Before you give
up
Before you give in
Nothing will be new
Nothing will change
I'll sit here alone and bored for the rest of the night
Waiting for a response that will never come
From a person who's long gone
Am I pathetic
For hoping
For dreaming
Is it wrong to imagine that the world will change
That this time it will be different
I've lost my train of thought
I've been waiting for so long

ACT 3- LOSING MYSELF

WAR OF THE HEART:

She was going through a war like no other
A war in her head with herself
Her mind had long been a battlefield
Grenades and mines strewn around with no thought to
consequence

Walking through the halls of her school was the equiva-
lent of a secret ops mission
She had to tip-toe carefully as not to alert either side to
her position

The taunting words of classmates hit her with the ferocity
of a small bomb
Leaving her heart full of holes and discarded shrapnel
The threats of her teachers hurting no less
If she can just get through the next hour
The next class
The next day
The next year
Maybe she'll be okay

But then hits the nuke
Waves of frustration and anguish hit her from one side
Then a second wave of despair and hopelessness
Mushrooms filling her sky
Blocking out the light

The ground starts to give from underneath
And all she can do is cling on for dear life
Hope it passes before the bell rings
Her teacher will be mad if she's late

She must find shelter before she falls apart
Her feet carry her to the bathroom

Muscle memory as her mind is far too gone to be of any
help
Lock the stall
Like the bolt on a rifle
Sit
Breath
Cry

Because that's all there is to do
Cry and wait it out
Pick the pieces back up once it's over
Salvage what you can

Then she splashes some water on her face
To clean away the last of the debris

Grab your bag and head to class
Don't let anyone know of the war
It's her life and her fight
Alone

PUZZLE PIECE:

I feel like a piece of a puzzle from the wrong box
I want to fit in
And people have tried to help me do so
They offered for me to join their group
Dress like them
Smile like them
Watch the shows they watch
But I always feel like an imposter
Like I'm just squeezing myself into a space that I don't
belong in
I'll never be a part of them

I've gone from group to group
Trying desperately to find where I belong
But I'm a little too round
Too square
Too deep
Too shallow
Too me

TV growing up always said that there's a place for
everyone
But if that's true
Will those without anyone eventually find each other
A group made of the missing pieces with nowhere else to
go

Or do we spend our whole lives searching for our perfect
spot
And it never really existed

ALONE:

I can't be the only one who feels these things
So why does it feel like I am
If everyone is wearing a mask
Then no one knows what they're supposed to look like
underneath

My mask is funny
My mask is smart
My mask loves to laugh and smile
My mask is unbreakable
It is brave and strong

But, I am not

I had thought she showed me under her mask
But that was just a second, more deceitful mask

I feel like I am lying when I wear it
But I am more afraid of what people will think when they
see what's underneath

Maybe then I could find someone who feels the same way

EMOTION PART 1:

Anger
Sadness
Grief
Guilt
Betrayal
Loneliness

All things we all feel
Human emotions we despise
One at a time we can handle them
Alone in a room full of friends and family
Sad in a place full of laughter
All-consuming anger
Asked to forgive
Guilt for something you never did
Betrayed by those you loved most
Grief over those you lost
Even though they stepped on you to get out

But what can you do when they all hit at once
A blinding white light of emotion
That drops you to your knees
And overrides your senses
With no explanation
No real reason

The only feeling coming through the fog of overstimulation is a need for it all to stop

But at the same time feeling nothing is just as bad
You become a shell of who you once were
Nothing can break through and life becomes pointless

EMOTION PART 2:

Hope
Joy
Peace
Laughter
Love
Fulfillment

How do we live without these things
Maybe we can't
Maybe we need these simple things to survive
These emotions can change how we live our lives
And how we look at the people around us

Each of us dreams of a future filled
With hope
With peace
With joy
With laughter
With love

Sadly not all of us get what we want
We can spend our whole lives looking and trying
But never get the pleasure
The satisfaction
Of fulfillment in the end

If that's the case
Then what's the point
Why should I keep trying
Why not let this emptiness consume me
Give in to the void

LOST:

My eyes are open
My senses alive
I can hear Mom making dinner in the kitchen
The soft hum of the sink
The popping of the water on the stove
I can smell Dads cigarettes from his room down the hall
A welcome scent of home and comfort

But I can't tell if I'm actually awake
I don't remember coming to after my nap
There's a fog over my eyes
And a cloud of nothingness surrounding my heart
I might as well have been a ghost floating through the
motions
Consciousness and thought drift in and out like the tides
in a storm

I'd love to be in a storm
To dance in the rain
To scream with the thunder
Maybe that's where I am
And my house is the dream
I can't tell which is real anymore

HUMANITY'S FLAW:

What makes us human?
    We feel
    We think
    We have a sense of right from wrong
    It's our compassion for others
    And our wanting to help

What makes us feel the way we do?
    Depression
    Anxiety
    Brain juices
    A need to fit in
    To do right
    To be the best version of ourselves

Are we doomed to be forever incomplete?
    Probably

Broken?
    Definitely

Can I move on and be a person again?
    No
The feelings of self-hatred and eternal darkness are
all-consuming

A CRY FOR HELP:

I woke up this morning in tears
It was 3:30 am
Half an hour after I had fallen asleep
Finally
I was surrounded by those that cared about me
Those who I called my friends
But as I jump awake
Tears streaming down my face
A silent call out to the one I loved still on my lips
I didn't think to ask any of them for help
One needed sleep more than the rest of us
One would have been mad if I woke them
One I didn't feel I deserved to be bothered by me
After I hadn't talked to them in so long
And had asked so much of them already
Call it anxiety
Call it fear
Call it insecurity
No matter its name
It was the one that kept me on my best friends bedroom
floor
Crying
Clutching myself for hours
Alone
I had planned my escape
Sneak out and walk home before anyone wakes up

But we had plans for later
What kind of friend would I be if I abandoned them
So instead I sat there
And I waited
Trusted that I'd get over myself

Believed that I would get better soon
Then the tears started to fall again

TOO MUCH:

I just can't do this anymore
It's too much
Too hard

My emotions take control
They own me
They consume me

They make it so I am no longer who I used to be
Who I want to be

I am my emotions
My anger
My stress
My concerns
My fear
My compassion
No longer am I me

I can't control myself anymore
I am a wreck
When I'm not crying
I'm yelling and screaming
When I'm not giving myself up to someone
I'm being selfish and only worried about myself

I watch my life as if behind a glass
Someone
Something
Has taken over the controls and I am helpless to fight
them

This is just how it is
I don't have the energy to fight it anymore
I am done

SURVIVE A WEEK:

Day one:
    Try your best
Day two:
    At least try
Day three:
    Get through the day
Day four:
    A few hours
Day five:
    What's the point...

ACT 4- HOPE FOR AN END

I saw no way out
No way that things could get any better
Everything around me is dark
All my thoughts were shaking and crumbling onto the
floor around me
I knew no love
I felt no trust
I needed a freedom life couldn't give me
But death might

LIMITLESS:

The trees grow high to the sky
Desperate to escape the ground that holds them captive
If only I could soar through the air like their branches
If only I could be free

I write things down to let my thoughts go free
In hopes one day I could follow them
And if I were to keep them locked away they would con-
sume me
The little that is left

Eventually my demons will leak from my veins
Spreading their darkness to everything I touch
I'm so worried about preserving the world around me that
I no longer care what happens to me in the process

I can't follow my dreams
I just want to fly
To never touch the ground unless that is what I want to
do
I want to live my own life
To be happy to make my own mistakes
To learn my own lessons
I need to be my own person and follow my own adventure

No responsibilities
No family
No requirements
Nothing to hold me back any longer

ACT 5- GIVING IN

Maybe my whole life is meant to feel this empty
Why should I keep fighting it if this is my destiny
My punishment for love and trust
I don't deserve those things
I knew that
I hoped for them anyway
And I was slaughtered for it
I am ugly
A freak
A fag
A queer
An anorexic
A blond
I am stupid
I am slow
I am broken
I come from broken
I have nothing
I deserve nothing
And I should have known that instead of fighting it

CRYING ISN'T ALWAYS UGLY:

A single tear slips out of her eye
Dripping down her cheek
Traveling across her chin
Tracing down her neck
Only to stop once it hits her chest
She lets them run free
Why bother hiding them
The pain was so clearly written on her face
So why keep it from the world

BREAKING POINT:

You can normally feel that moment
The moment everything breaks

You feel your heart tear
The dam behind your eyes crashes
Your resolve crumbles
Sometimes it is not as bad as others
Sometimes it's slow and you can feel it coming
In moments like that you can get away and be alone to
hold yourself

But it's the moments where it comes on all at once
One minute you're fine and you feel strong
The next everything starts to crash and burn
There's no longer any hope to put yourself back together
What's the point in even trying

Every
"Are you okay?
What's wrong? "
is another new nail in the coffin
You don't need them
They don't understand
They don't even try

People don't want to help you
They feel obligated
They just want to ask so they don't feel guilty later
You've heard it all before
And not one of them sticks around once you've calmed

You just need to be alone
When you're alone you can let it all out
You don't need to trust someone not to stab you in the
back
All you ever need is yourself

I'M ABOUT TO GO TO SLEEP

But I felt I should write something first
I haven't done this in such a long time
And it's getting so late
I've been so tired lately
For no reason
Maybe it's the weather
Or it could be my meds
I could blame it on school work
Or the way my family is falling apart
Maybe I'm just another spoiled goth writer Hoping some-
one will listen
Or another kid lost in the sea
Reaching for someone to pull me out and save me
I don't know
I probably never will
All I can do is sleep it off
Hope I feel better in the morning
Goodnight cold moon
Goodnight cold breeze
Goodnight dark thoughts that will follow me into my
dreams

HELPLESS:

I hate this emotional up and down
Happy to sad
Exhausted then energized
Hours where I can't move to more hours where I can't
sleep
It surrounds everyday

I want help
It's not that I think this is okay
Or normal
But I can't tell you how to help me
Because I don't know what I need
But, God do I wish I did

You can try all you want
You can poke and prod me as much as you like
You can spend the next forever looking for answers
But I can't be fixed

And part of me doesn't want to be
There's nothing wrong with me
I like being broken in my own way
My chips and cracks are part of who I am

If I can't find who I'm supposed to be in this world
Maybe it's because I already found it

I'm here to be sad
To be helpless
To be broken
Because it gives purpose to those around me

I was put here to be this abomination
And God damn it I'm going to be
I'm a whore for the attention
Nothing brings people in like a freak show

So let me be
Stop trying to fix me
I don't want your help
And even if I did
There's nothing to be done
This is just what I am

WHY?

The unexplained feeling of being alone in a crowd of
people
The feeling of being tired while still wide awake
The feeling of just wanting to close your eyes and never
open them again
The feeling of wanting to be held and wanting to be left
to cry by yourself
The need to listen to sad music to help cheer you up
The hatred of people who are laughing and being happy
While you have to work so hard to feel anything

Why?
Why is this happening to me?
Is this some kind of cosmic joke?
I loved the wrong person and didn't believe in God so this
is my punishment?!

If there really was an all-loving God then why the fuck is
he torturing me
Shouldn't he be all about forgiveness and repentance
I don't deserve this!

Take it back
Please
I can't hold on any longer

I just want love
Unquestioning
Without any ties or bull shit criteria to meet

I need these emotions to let up
To feel things how I used to
While there's still any of me left

BEHIND THE SECRETS:

No one would ever know it was me
I could hide behind the lies and secrets
They never really knew me anyway
Now they never will

THE HOSPITAL:

It's cold without my proper clothes
I almost wish I hadn't told anyone how I was feeling
The hospital is packed today
It's almost funny
If I had gone through with it they probably would have
had a hard time saving me
With so many car accidents today
But I couldn't
I gave in
I was too much a coward to even kill myself right

But maybe it's for the best
Maybe this will change things
Something
Anything
And if not I can always try again

What if I don't want to though
Now I know that they actually care
My mom won't stop crying.
My dad is at a loss
I don't even know where he is
Have they told my brother yet
What will he think of me
I'm supposed to watch over him
And I was going to leave him and everyone else behind

I thought it would be easier for them.
One less mouth to feed
One less thing to worry about
Their plates are already so full
At least a little bit

Mom is trying her best
It's not her fault she's only working with partial truths and
half of the story

I feel scared
I feel guilty
I feel so far away from everything that's going on
But at least I can feel Something

ACT 6- HOPE FOR THE FUTURE

You can't heal in a day
No one can
It takes time
I took some time off from writing
I had to find myself again
They put me on some medications to help
And sometimes it did

It takes time for love and self-acceptance
I had to learn
That I am all of the things that are wrong with me
But I am also so much more

I will work through this
I will move on
I will heal
I will find a way to get up each morning
A way for myself
I will become my own anchor
But the first step was reaching out for help again
And relearning to trust
I will still have bad days
And that's okay
As long as I don't focus on them
As long as I keep moving forward

NEVERENDING:

A story can start any way you want it to
Maybe instead of a depressed teenager
Your narrator is…
I don't know
A unicorn?
A pigeon?
OH!
A penguin!

And this penguin lives a happy life with all its penguin
friends
Together they go on great adventures with grand happy
endings
Maybe that would be a better story to tell
But it wouldn't be the truth

The truth is a lot has happened lately
Life has some good moments now
My parents have been spending a lot more time with me
And I don't feel like I have to lie to them all the time
anymore

There are still bad days
The days when the meds aren't enough to keep all the old
feelings at bay
But they aren't as bad anymore

And it's nice to know I can still feel things every once in a
while

I still have days of total darkness though
Days where thoughts of suicide rise up in the back of my
mind
Like a taunting prize waiting to be won

But I have people for that now
My therapist is very nice
She likes listening to my writing
And hearing me go on and on about books

But there's still this shadow lingering over me
A fear that this is all a dream
That it'll all come crashing back down
It's not always easy to ask for help
Loneliness is a hard habit to break
And what if once I ask for help
Everything becomes fine again
I'd be the girl who cried depression
Believing it's there when it's not

I MET SOMEONE NEW:

And I know what you're thinking
But not this time
His name is John
He is patient
Kind
Stable
And he loves me
He tells me so
Every time he has the chance
He isn't shy
He makes me laugh
He makes me smile again
It's been so long
I missed it

It's long-distance for now
He's off at college
But that might be even better for me
It gives me space
And time
To adjust
To breath

He is more than willing to wait for me
To listen
To understand

It's going to take me a while to tell it all
But he's excited to hear it
He accepts my baggage
He understands that one doesn't come without the other
He's exactly what I need

BROKEN:

Maybe I'm too broken to feel anything anymore
My limits were tested over and over
Until every last one was passed
Until I had nothing left
And now you're here
You wonder why I can't seem to trust you
Why it's hard for me to give in
Well here's your answer
Every time I did
I felt what it means to break in a new way
Part of me wants to believe you won't do that
But I'm down to my last life
I can't give that to you
Not yet

But I'm working on it
I know
Deep down
That you mean me no harm
That you'll love me and cherish me
But things happen
I just need more time

JOHN:

2:08 Am
I wish you were here
I wish for your arms around my body
I wish to lay with you under the covers
The only thing between us is our underwear as we heat
each other through the winter night
It's so cold without you here

The wind grins at me with its ominous chill
It knows how much I miss your warmth
And mocks me for it

It somehow knows that I can't do anything to stop it
That I will lay here
Forever
Embracing its frigid solitude
Until you come to save me
I am a princess locked in her tower
Helplessly trapped
Waiting for a savior

I can dream of a world where I don't need you
But it would quickly become a nightmare
Without your light
Without your warmth

IF YOU WERE HERE:

If you were here
    I'd sing you a song
    I'd tell you a story
    We'd laugh
    I'd cry
    You'd hold me

If you were here
    I'd curl in close
    I'd rest my head on your chest
    We'd cling to each other
    I'd never let go
    You'd pull me closer

If you were here
    I'd love you forever
    I'd never take my eyes off of you
    We'd fall for each other endlessly
    I'd be your asylum
    You'd be my safety

NIGHTMARE:

I still wake up sometimes
No air in my lungs
Fear in my heart

John holds me
He kisses my head and tells me everything will be okay
My past is gone
All that is left is him
Our little family

I still scream into the night
I wake up with my face wet with tears

Some mornings
John will kiss my forehead
Or rub my back
And I jump awake
Afraid of his touch
Not knowing yet that he isn't one of the monsters follow-
ing me out of my dreams

But he doesn't mind
He holds me tight
Brushes my hair
Rocks me back to sleep

It isn't perfect
I don't want perfect
I want to feel and be happy
And that's what I have

I AM:

I am Beautiful
I am Smart
I am Brave
I am Kind
I am Trusting
I am Loving
I am Fragile
I am Silly
I am Creative
I am a Scatterbrain
I am a Little Crazy
And all of that is Okay
Because I am Human

CONCLUSION-

Writing has always been an outlet for me to best express myself. I have always had some kind of journal or notebook on me, ever since middle school.

Once I had turned eighteen I started noticing some pain in my legs every once in a while. At first, everyone told me they were delayed growing pains, then it was just stress from my job and my long distance relationship. In January of 2019, I stopped being able to walk without exorbitant amounts of pain in both of my legs and pain in my arms and back.

My doctor called it Fibromyalgia.

A chronic pain syndrome in the joints.

I was nineteen.

They said it was from an excess of stress in my life. Constant strain on the tissue and brain from anxiety. I knew I had a rough time in high school. I had been to a hospital on suicide watch and was put on some different medications to try and take care of it.

But now I can't have a normal life. I can't be a reckless twenty-something. And it's happening all the time now. To kids like me. So I want to tell my story, through the poems I wrote in high school while everything was happening. To both warn people, and to let them know that eventually, it can get better.

CPSIA information can be obtained
at www.ICGtesting.com
Printed in the USA
LVHW081953310321
682892LV00037B/1993